Till 21 Years Old !!

A poetry collection of emotions till 21 years old

Dr Ajithraa JK

BookLeaf Publishing

India | USA | UK

Made with ❤ on the BookLeaf Publishing Platform
www.bookleafpub.in
www.bookleafpub.com

Dedication

Dedicated to all humans who crossed my life and sparked poetic fantasy of my brain !!!

Preface

Creativity have always been a beautiful feeling and may a defensive mask to escape from the reality and get submerged in the joy of fantasy desires. The one such creativity would be poetry where words are scribbled not just by pens but by heart and transformed it into an emotion to cherish memories!!

As i started writing poems by age 10, which were actually just scribbles on some simple topics but the moments of creating a masterpiece have always been sparking my creative mind shiner and shiner !! And as i grew up, the desire to publish this treasure of different emotions just gave me a contended feeling of living a mindful life. So, here am with collection of poems that i wrote at different age with different perspectives of life and changes.

And wish the readers dwell in the joy of experiencing evitable emotions of one's life !!
Happy reading !

Acknowledgements

Am grateful to my biggest pillar of support Dr Gowtham who is my husband, who consistently support me not to lose my identity of who am.

A big thank you to my sweetest daughter Aadhira GA for understanding this poetic mom and giving me space to write this book.

Thank you dear parents Mr.Johnson and Mrs Kanaga Bai for being more supportive through out.

Thank you Dr Shyam Sundar who is my friend, who shares similar poetic human nature and discussing poetry with him have always been encouraging.

Thank you Book leaf publishing for making this dream book into reality.

1. THE RAIN

Sitting in the dawn of evening,
Looking for friends to play,
A loneliness encircled me;
oh yeah !! i could not find anyone here !!
My heart is feeling dull and empty ,
Weeping for play time !!

As the dawn darkens,
The leaves are falling slow,
Drops of rain touched me,
Like a pearl of string,
Gave me hope of Joy,
oh yeah !! its Raining , Raining !!!

My heart jumped into smiles,
And danced in happiness!!
Drenched in beauty of RAIN !!

2. THE TSUNAMI

Hey Tsunami,
In the coasts of Sea,
Everyone were living a life of poverty,
With a family of love,

Hey Tsunami,
Why are you angry ?
Why are your waves so high ?
Scaring those innocent humans !!

Hey Tsunami,
Why are you violent ?
Why are your waves so destructive?
Taking the Lives of vulnerable humans !!

Hey Tsunami,
Why are you unheard?
Why are yours waves so rushing?
Ignoring the cry of endangered humans !!

3. HE THE LORD

Oh, The Almighty, The Almighty,
Up above the sky,
He stands like a Majestic Moon,
His holiness shines everywhere !!

Oh, The Almighty, The Almighty,
He rise as Sparkling Shine,
Spreading us ray of Hope,
To fight battles each day !!

Oh, The Almighty, The Almighty,
He blossoms as a sweet fragnance,
Adding joy to one's life,
To keep our nerves calm !!

Oh, The Almighty, The Almighty,
He is the saviour of our existence,
Making us stronger and bolder,
To live this life happier and happier !!

4. LIFE IS A MAGIC

Life is a Magic,
Oh, Life is a Magic !
When your little little heart,
Searches for little little Joy,
It engraves pearls of happiness ;
But, when you need it forever,
It dumps your heart broken !!
When you don't need a lesson,
It will teach you everyday;
You may lose what your soul desires,
But, may come back with surprises !!
Because, "Life is a Magic "!!!

5. FRIENDSHIP IS MY TREASURE

Sitting in my loneliness,
Thinking of our friendship,
I admire the golden threads,
That bind our hearts together,
To share our thoughts together !!

Our Friendship blossoms,
Like a beautiful flower ;
I admire the destiny,
For giving me a precious gift,
To keep as a everlasting treasure !!

I put a eternal favour,
To the Universe of God,
To have us in His juicy bound,
As Best Friends Forever !!!

6. HATE YOU CIGARETTES

Hey, Hate you, Hate you ever !!
You are a killing sweetheart,
Oh, cigarettes, you mesmerize us ,
But, you are a silent killer !!

Hey, Hate you, Hate you ever !!
You are weapon destroying souls,
Oh, cigarettes, you give pleasure,
But, you are a life spoiler !!

Hey, Hate you, Hate you ever !!
Hate you cigarettes !!

7. NEED A WORLD TO LIVE

Yes, I need a world,
Where I could admire,
Nature's serenity !!

Yes, I need a world,
Where I could fly,
With Right freedom !!

Yes, I need a world,
Where my words,
Can heal people !!

Yes, I need a world,
Where I could have ,
Space for the best one's !!

Yes, I need a world,
Where I could melt,
Only with music !!

Yes, I need a world,
Where I could live ,
And stop existing !!!

8. SHADES OF LIFE

When Shades of life,
Fade away,
Like a shadow;
When Colours of life,
Pass away,
Like a cloud;
Listen to your heart ,
And it still beats alive !!

9. BAD TOUCH

Bad touch ! Bad touch !!
Feels embarrassing ;
Why not Good touch ?

Chaotic ! Chaotic !!
Feels confusing ;
Why not Confident ?

Ignorance ! Ignorance !!
Feels losing,
Why not Sex education ?

Whisper ! Whisper !!
Feels regretting ;
Why not Loud ?

Tears ! Tears !!
Feels mourning,
Why not "SAY NO" ?

10. A CREDIT TO ENRIQUE SONGS

My heart skips a beat,
When i hear your music beats,
As shower of rain,
Your music drench me completely !

Your humming,
Takes me away,
Out of reality !!

Oh, Hero of music !!
Your words are so deep,
Stealing everybody's heart,
I fly like Angel of Heaven !!

11. LIFE IS A WONDERFUL LIE

When I believed promises,
Life taught me lies,
When perfection defined me,
Life made me imperfect,
When I searched for shoulders,
Only my shadows are left ;
When Iam fed up,
Opportunities knocked me,
When i desired for my dreams,
Reality popped me up,
When I left things to Destiny,
I was crowned with Decision making !!
Yes, Life is a WONDERFUL LIE,

12. MOMS LOVE

As life goes on,
Time would run away,
Only with flashbacks,
Days would shut down,
Only with memories,
Relationships would fade,
Only with pains;

But, Oh, Human, Oh, Human,
There will be a love ,
So stronger than you believe;
There will be a heart ,
So pure than you see,
That Glory heart is your MOM !!!

13. THE HIDING STAINS

Like a little angel of nature,
I was a happy free go girl,
Cherishing each day!!

But that one day,
Oh no !! Ouch !!
Stomach is aching !!

Yeah !! the Red stains!!
My First Periods !!
Left me with Ruins !!

Shhh !! Shh !! Shhh!!
Why should I ?
Keep it as Hiding stains !!

14. THE MOURNING

She is a beautiful Angel,
In the shades of night,
Her tears fell down,
As twinkling stars ,
In the dark sky !!

She weeped, weeped,
As a River of water
Until the Sun,
Sparkled again !!

15. FALLING IN LOVE

When thunder met lightening,
The storm appeared fierce,
In the chaos of Heavy Rain,
With no clue to survival,
I Met this man of hearts!
Who stole my heart ,
To be my SAVIOUR !!

16. SURVIVAL

As my heart grows,
With turns and turns of Changes,
Broken !! Broken !! Broken !!
Only to be beautiful ,
In a World Of Survival !!

17. HUMAN VAMPIRES

Six headed !! Six headed !!
yeah ! six headed senses we are !!
Sin headed !! Sin headed !!
yeah !! Sin headed we are !!
Senseless !! Senseless !!
Yeah !!Senseless we are !!
Selfish !! Selfish !!
Yeah !! Selfish we are !!

18. ETERNITY

Eternity !! Eternity !!
Am looking for you;
My Everlasting eternity,
My Long lasting eternity !!
Searching you,
In the roof of mountains,
In the universe of stars,
In the joy of smiles,
In the victory of achievements,
In the Love of humans !!
Oh !! Eternity !! Eternity !!
But I Found you,
Inside me, Inside me,
Only inside myself !!

19. THE FIERCE

Dedication to one of my childhood friend who passed away !!!

Run ,Run ,Run !!
He ran like a LEOPARD,
In the athletic track;

Power, Power, Power !!
He is powerful like a LION,
In the athletic track;

Fierce, Fierce , Fierce !!
He took his life,
In the failure of his desires !!!

20. CURING MINDS

Searching meaning,
Of my existence,
Admired and dwelled,
In the Universe of life !!!

Happiness was not complete,
Until I learnt ,
Curing INSANE minds !!

21. RESILIENCE

Broken,
Betrayed,
Disappointed,
Saddened,
Frustrated,
Miserable,

were part of myself ,
Until, I learnt,
The art of Resilience !!!